LEADERSHIP....
Rules of Engagement

Tim L. Holman
PO Box 353
North Hampton, Ohio 45349
(937) 964-1534
htdholman@donet.com

Copyright © 2002

Tim L. Holman
PO Box 353
North Hampton, Ohio 45349

All rights reserved.

Library of Congress Control Number:
2002090140

ISBN:
978-0-9715251-0-8

Printed in the United States by
Morris Publishing
3212 East Highway 30
Kearney, NE 68847
1-800-650-7888

Table Of Contents

Page 2	Provide the focus.
Page 4	Leadership is a privilege.
Page 6	The attitude of the leader will set the tone.
Page 8	Expect to be challenged.
Page 10	What ever you allow becomes the standard.
Page 12	You can't lead if you don't care.
Page 14	Remember the Ten Commandments.
Page 16	You can't lead where you can't see.
Page 18	You will make mistakes.
Page 20	Your success is in direct proportion to the success of the people.
Page 22	Deal in facts not assumptions.
Page 24	Pull the people don't push.
Page 26	Change perceptions and you change attitudes.
Page 28	Be part of the team.
Page 30	Empower the people.
Page 32	Listen more than you talk.
Page 34	Celebrate success.
Page 36	The customer is not always right.
Page 38	Ride the currents of change.
Page 40	Never stop learning.
Page 42	Some people never grow up.
Page 44	Pick your battles carefully.
Page 46	Counseling does not have to be adversarial.
Page 48	Teach yourself out of a job.
Page 50	Leadership is not about ego.

Rule # 1

Provide the focus.

The most common cause of team burnout or team ineffectiveness is lack of focus. The focus is made up of the *mission, vision, and goals* of the organization. These are not just fancy statements placed on a piece of paper and hung on the wall. They are well defined documents that are lived on a daily basis. Every employee's action should be in direct support of these documents.

Mission describes the purpose. Vision describes the future or where you want to be. And the goals provide the how.

Whenever possible get the employee involved in helping develop these documents to help increase the ownership within the organization.

If the leader fails to provide a focus....the employee will develop their own focus. That focus will be centered around the employee and not the organization. This leads to performance issues and ineffective teams.

To enhance this concept the leader should also review the job description and expectations with every employee. The employee must understand how their work impacts the organization.

Remember light becomes a powerful laser only when the light is focused. Focused energy is powerful energy. So keep the people focused.

Rule # 2

Leadership is a privilege!

Leadership is a great privilege. To be in a position to lead others is a tremendous responsibility. The leader must never lose sight of the importance of their position.

As a leader, you chose to be in this position. You asked to be in a leadership capacity. No one forced you to take the position. So if you want to be a leader, do it to the best of your ability.

Understand that many people depend on you, your actions, and your decisions. You have the ability to impact a number of people in a positive or negative way. Choose to make a positive impact.

Leadership is a privilege because you have influence over people. They look to you for guidance and answers. The people look to the leader in time of adversity to see how they will react. The leader's response under pressure will determine the response of the people.

The leader has the opportunity, a purpose for people who have never had purpose. The leader has the opportunity to take people to a new level of performance. The leader has the opportunity to make people better than they were yesterday. Leadership is *all* about people.

Remember, leadership is a privilege. Don't abuse it. *Leadership must be handled with care.*

Rule # 3

The attitude of the leader will set the tone for the organization.

What attitude do you bring to the organization? Are you negative? Do you talk about other members of the organization? Or, are you positive and supportive? Do you build up or do you tear down? Do you look for opportunity in adversity or do you complain about everything?

As a leader your attitude sets the tone for the people you lead. Their attitude is, in many cases, a direct reflection of the leader.

Attitude will make or break a team. If the leader is negative it is very difficult for the people to be positive.

Attitude is the one thing that people have total control over. The leader can choose his/her attitude. So, choose to have a positive one.

The attitude of an organization will make it better or it will destroy it. Attitude impacts morale. Morale impacts productivity, quality, turnover and absenteeism.

Maintaining a positive attitude is not always an easy task. But success as a leader is very dependent on it. Not a Polly Anna attitude but, an attitude that is constantly working to improve the organization. An attitude that says we have problems, but together we can fix most problems.

Remember, the leader with the right attitude is the *solution,* not the problem.

Rule # 4

Expect to be challenged.

A good leader is not afraid to make decisions. They gather as much information that is available and they make their call.

Sometimes the leader has very little information to go on. But knowing a decision must be made they stand up to the task and make the call.

The leader will make mistakes. And at times they will make the wrong call. When this happens you can expect someone to play Monday morning quarterback and criticize your decision. Expect it!

Even when the leader makes a good call there will be those who will not agree and they will challenge any and all decisions. As a leader you must rise above it.

If the leader hesitates to make decisions because someone may challenge them, the leader becomes ineffective.

Base your decision on sound data whenever possible. Admit when you are wrong and be eager to fix your mistakes.

Remember, everyone has a better way after the fact. As a leader you will be called to make quick decisions with little on no information. Make the decision that you think will be best for the organization and *expect to be challenged.*

Rule # 5

Whatever you allow becomes the standard.

Allow an individual to clock in fifteen minutes late for several weeks and soon this is the acceptable standard. Set your standards high. Not so high that it is impossible for people to reach them, but high enough that they receive a sense of accomplishment when the standard is reached.

If the leader allows people to drift from the set standard he or she may be sending out a message of apathy. And inadvertently the leader is lowering the standard over time.

Standards are important because they give the people a target to shoot for. It allows them to stay focused and to make a positive impact on the organization. Without standards some may do just enough to get by. This is not acceptable. The people are there to help you move the organization ahead. To make it better than it was yesterday.

Don't allow mediocre performance set the standards with input from the people. Understand what impacts their performance and provide whatever they need to do the job well.

Remember, whatever you allow becomes the standard, so allow high performance.

Rule # 6

You can't lead if you don't care.

Leadership is about caring for the people and the organization. If you don't care, you need to get out of the leadership position. There are far too many people in leadership roles that care a great deal for themselves but very little for the people.

The leaders greatest asset is the people. The people will make the leader look very good or very bad. If the leader cares about the people and takes good care of them they will, in turn, take care of the leader.

It may seem hard to care about some in the organization, but everyone has value. And everyone has something to contribute. Look for ways they can contribute and help them succeed.

Develop performance based reward systems that recognize the people for a job well done. Emphasize the good. Don't ignore weaknesses or poor performance. Deal with it. But place more emphasis on the positive.

Show the people you care about them. Show them that you are willing to stand behind them and support them.

Remember, treat others the way you want to be treated......*it's not rocket science!*

Rule # 7

Remember the Ten Commandments.

Sound principles are the foundation of leadership. The Ten Commandments provides the value system that has stood firm for many years.

Moses lead scores of people across the wilderness with the Ten Commandments as the rules to live by.

Without a baseline for what is right and wrong, the leader may be tempted to define *right* as what is best for the leader instead of what's best for the organization. All leaders must answer to a higher authority. And the Ten Commandment can provide the checks and balances needed to do that which is right.

The Ten Commandments can help maintain the leaders integrity even when the pressure is on. Compromise your integrity and you lose credibility. Lose your credibility and you lose your ability to lead.

Strong values and principles provide the guiding light for the leader. Our Creator provided us with these commandments so everyone would have a baseline for right and wrong.

Remember, they are the Ten Commandments, not the ten suggestions.

Rule # 8

You can't lead where you can't see. And you can only lead as far as you can see.

Vision is seeing clearly what could be. Vision allows us to go beyond today. It allows us to expand our horizons.

Every great leader throughout history has had the gift of vision. Having vision is only the first step, communicating that vision so everyone can see it is the second step.

John F. Kennedy had a vision to place a man on the moon. His vision was carried out even after his death because he was able to communicate his vision to others. He had the ability to get the people to stand behind his vision.

The size of your accomplishments, the quality of your achievement depends largely on the size of your vision. The leader goes where their vision is and no further. Great leaders have great visions. Small leaders have small visions.

The vision is a dream. So dream big. You may never reach your vision but you will constantly strive for it. You are moving closer to it day after day. Even if you never reach your vision you are still better because you tried.

Vision is creating the future. To design the ideal and to move into the future with a map.

Remember, *create* your vision, *communicate* your vision, get the people *excited* about your vision.

Rule # 9

You will make mistakes!

Even great leaders make mistakes from time to time. How they handle these mistakes will determine their future as a leader. If mistakes pull you down to the point that you are unable to recover, your success as a leader is jeopardized.

It is impossible to make the right decision in every case. The lack of information and changing dynamics makes it next to impossible to make the right choice 100% of the time.

The leader has several choices when they make a mistake. They can deny the mistake was made and place the blame on others, thus creating an atmosphere of distrust. Or they can accept responsibility for the mistake and learn from it. This in turn enhances the trust within the organization and increases the leaders credibility.

When the leader views a mistake as a learning opportunity, the leader analyses the error to determine how it was made and how it could be approached next time. This creates a continuous learning mentality.

Never confuse a mistake or a failure of a task for failure of life. If you would have quit after your first attempt at walking you would still be crawling on all fours.

Remember, most success is preceded by mistakes and or failures.

Rule # 10

Your success is in direct proportion to the success of the people.

"You can burn my buildings but if you give me my people I can build them right back again." Henry Ford made that statement because he understood how important the people are. People are the leader's greatest asset. No other resource is more important.

No leader can be a success without people. The number one goal of any leader should be to help the people succeed. If the people succeed, the organization succeeds. If the organization succeeds, the leader succeeds.

Failure to recognize and adopt this rule will result in productivity, morale, attendance, and turnover issues. The leader is only as strong as the people they lead.

A group of highly motivated people led by a strong leader can accomplish just about anything. Leaders recognize the strengths of their people and capitalize on them.

The old saying that leadership is a lonely position is only true when this rule is ignored. Strong leaders are surrounded by many strong followers. Together they create great things.

Remember, the leader is only as strong as the people they lead.

Rule # 11

Deal in facts not assumptions.

Successful leaders seek out the facts. They are not satisfied with hearsay, rumors or gossip. They look for and rely on accurate data. Decisions are made much easier when there is sound data available.

If the leader is influenced by rumors and gossip, inappropriate actions are taken and the credibility of the leader is impacted.

The next time someone comes to you, upset over something they have heard, ask them what they know for sure. What are the facts?

Failure to deal in facts can create turmoil and chaos in any organization. The leader must communicate the data that the people need to do their jobs effectively.

Teach the people where to find the information they need. Over communicate. Provide a big picture of the organization. Make it easy to get information.

Open book management is an excellent way to lead an organization. Open book management means that all information is available to employees. There are no secrets except for employee disciplinary action and counseling.

Dealing in facts actually helps reduce the rumor mill since everyone is on the same page and they have an abundance of information at their fingertips.

Remember, taking action based on facts will provide optimal results.

Rule # 12

Pull the people, don't push.

A basketball coach decided to change the offensive plays for the team. This was a total revamping of the play book. Most of the players had spent many hours learning the old plays and they were not too excited about learning a whole new set of plays.

As the coach introduced the new changes some of the players were resistant to them. Some did not vocalize their concern, but during practice it was obvious their heart was not in it.

In this case the coach continued to pull his players through the change. He would talk frequently about why the change was needed and how each player would benefit. Then they would go back to practice and the coach would lead them step by step through each play. Over time the players became comfortable with the plays and more supportive of them.

In this example the coach could have become very authoritarian and pushed the new play book on the players. After all he is the coach and he makes the rules. Instead the coach was patient. At no time did he back off. He stayed focused and pulled the people along. The longer he pulled, less effort and energy was required for movement until, finally, the players were moving in the right direction on their own.

Remember, pulling the people requires the leader to be *out front clearing the trail.*

Rule # 13

Change perceptions and you will change attitudes.

Ever wonder why repeated counseling doesn't change behavior? A supervisor had an employee who was tardy everyday for two weeks. He called the individual in for counseling. His tardiness stopped.

Several weeks later the supervisor noticed that the same employee was calling off work on a regular basis. The supervisor calls the individual in and again counseled him. The call ins stopped.

As time went on the supervisor was noticing this same employee's work productivity and quality were decreasing. Frustrated the supervisor once again called the individual in for counseling.

Long term behavior changes only come when the individual's perceptions change. Perceptions are not developed overnight and they are not changed overnight.

Perceptions are the way a person views the world. Negative views lead to negative behaviors. Positive views lead to positive behaviors. Change the perception and you change attitudes. Change attitudes and long term behavior changes will be seen.

The leader changes behaviors by focusing the individual on the *truth*. Show the person the facts, what is real, and life in general may not be as bad as it appears on the surface.

Remember, change the *perception* and you will change *attitudes* and *behavior*.

Rule # 14

Be part of the team.

Being part of the team means the leader will make a difference. Making a difference isn't just telling the team what to do. It's not just going through the motions. It means the leader does the the things for the team that makes a positive impact. It is doing what counts.

The leadership position doesn't guarantee the leader will contribute in a positive way. The leader must stay close to the team and understand the needs of the team.

The leader must concentrate on providing the team with the needs in a timely manner. It must add value to the team process.

To be a team player the leader must monitor team effectiveness. Pay attention to the group and recognize and deal with problems before they happen. Look for ways the team can improve. Look for individuals who need your support and encouragement.

The leader must build a climate of trust. The team grows as trust grows. If team members can't trust the leader they will never trust other members or the team process. Focus on the small stuff that will help nurture the team trust level.

Remember, the team leader, does just that, *leads*. The leader must set the example for the group......*they must be part of the team.*

Rule # 15

Empower the people.

The leader cannot do all that needs to be done. As stated earlier, the success of the leader is dependent on the people. Therefore the people must be empowered to carry out their jobs with the ability to make decisions.

There are three components that need to be present to empower people. First they must be given *responsibility*.

Next they must be given the *authority* to make decisions concerning the responsibility. Parameters are set and the individual can make all decisions within those parameters. As they mature in the empowering process the parameters are expanded.

The third element of empowerment is accountability. Accountability does not mean punishment. It means if one team player drops the ball he or she understands how it effects every other team member. Accountability is knowing how our individual actions effect the team as a whole. Drop the ball over and over, then discipline may be needed.

Empowerment allows the leader to become stronger. It does not take power away from the leader, it enhances it.

Empowerment makes the group more effective which in turn makes the leader more effective.

Remember, empowerment is a *process* that *grows* with the leader.

Rule # 16

Listen more than you talk.

Most people will agree that they are not good communicators. The leader must work to become an excellent communicator. To communicate better the leader must be a good listener. Many people think that communicating is based mainly on talking. But this is not true. Listening is the most important element of communications.

There are two types of listening. There is passive listening and there is active listening.

Passive listening is voluntary and requires very little effort. Listening to music as you drive is an example of passive listening.

Active listening requires effort. Information is processed and details are obtained. Listening to a lecture that will be followed by a test is an example of active listening.

The leader must make sure they are in the active listening mode at the right times. Being in the passive mode when you should be in the active mode will assure disaster.

If the leader is unable to develop excellent listening skills, they will be unable to determine the needs and problems of the people. This can lead to apathy by the people and poor morale will follow.

Remember, God gave us two ears and one mouth so we would listen twice as much as we talk. Listen to the people.

Rule # 17

Celebrate success.

Emphasize the positive. Don't ignore the problems, just put more emphasis on the positive.

A company was very proud of the fact that they had the best month in their twenty five year history. They exceeded both sales and production goals. When the CEO of the organization was asked what they did to celebrate their success, he responded with, "Nothing!"

When the same CEO was asked what he would do if the company had the lowest sales and production month in their history he said, "I would call the people together and talk to them about the problem." Unfortunately this is a common mentality in many organizations. If they fail, someone will be there to criticize. But no one says much when the team is successful.

To change this mind set, the leader needs to look for success in the organization and be prepared to celebrate that success. It doesn't require much money to celebrate. Just be innovative and see what you can come up with.

One of the best rewards you can give is a thank you card sent to the individuals home address. It is personal, it shows that you took the time to recognize them and it has meaning.

Remember, *sneak* around and catch people doing good things. Then *reward* them.

Rule # 18

The customer is not always right.

For many years business owners have said that the customer is always right. Although this concept sounds good, it is not true. There are times when the customer, both internal and external, are wrong. To act like they are right when they are actually wrong can set the tone for many problems.

Let's say your company charges $49.95 for an item that it produces. A customer comes to your business and says that the product is only worth $10. Is the customer right? Will you sell the product to the for $10 and lose $39.95? If you do, chances are you will not be in business very long.

No, the customer is not always right. But, the customer always has the *right to be heard and understood*. This means the leader will listen to the customer with empathy. The leader will try to understand the situation, not from their own point of view, but from the customers point view.

Active listening helps build relationships, trust, and understanding. The effective leader must understand their customers. They may not always agree with them, but they do understand them.

Remember, if the leader takes care of the internal customer, the internal customer will be more likely to listen and understand the external customer.

Rule # 19

Ride the currents of change!

The leader must engage the future, see change as opportunity, and design the new. There is no need to fear change. Change will occur with or without you.

As an effective leader, change should be viewed as an ally. It is a tool to make the organization better today than it was yesterday.

Change provides opportunity, creates new processes, new services, new products and new views.

Most fear related to change comes from those who are not prepared. They have failed to plan and anticipate change. This results in a very reactive response to the change process.

Effective leaders keep their ear to the ground and they see change coming. They plan for the change process.

Managing and implementing change is much easier when the leader involves the people. The people should be involved in the design process. They will fear and resist less if they play a part in creating the new.

Most resistance to the change process is due to the change being dumped in the people's lap. Involving the the people early in the process prevents this resistance.

Remember, change is the design tool that creates tomorrow.

Rule # 20

Never stop learning!

Learning is a life long process. Leaders are constantly learning. They learn from the people they lead, from reading, from seminars, from school and most importantly they learn from their mistakes.

Once a leader stops the learning process he or she become less effective. A leader that stays current and is always obtaining new information has a competitive edge.

A college degree is not necessary to be educated. But the mind needs to be constantly stimulated to stay active and healthy. This can be accomplished by reading thought provoking material or attending seminars that provide information that can be use in our daily activity.

Life experiences are also valuable tools that can educate the leader. The leader should be learning something new each and everyday. Some days will result in success while other days result in mistakes. Both situations can be used as tools for learning.

Once the leader stops learning, the leader becomes stagnant. Stagnant leads to complacency. Complacency leads to burnout and ineffectiveness.

Remember, if we are too old to learn we are too old to lead. Never stop learning.

Rule # 21

Some people never grow up!

Some people grow old but they never grow up. So you might say we have some old kids in organizations.

The truth is maturity levels will vary greatly among employees. Some are very mature and have great work ethic, while other are very immature and have poor work ethic.

Don't be fooled by the so called generation X theory. In many case age has little to do with maturity. Some young employees may have excellent work ethic while some fifty or sixty year old employees have very poor work ethic.

It's unfortunate but in many cases the leader will have to teach the type of work ethic that is expected. Start right from the interview and let employees know what the acceptable behavior looks like on a daily basis. When the employee varies from the expected, coach their performance back to the acceptable level.

Immature employees with poor work ethic require high maintenance from the leader. If after a reasonable amount of coaching the employees performance is not acceptable, it may be time to terminate the employee (dehire).

Remember, don't ignore the immature employee, hoping that they will improve, deal with them in a firm but fair manner.

Rule # 22

Pick your battles carefully!

You are the leader of a group of great employees. They work well together and have developed into a cohesive team. Unfortunately, your boss is not too supportive of you or your team. You have talked to him about the way you feel on several occasions but nothing has changed. When should you go to the next level in the chain of command?

This scenario is not uncommon in some organizations and the leader must be careful in how he or she handles the situation.

Pick your battles carefully. Then decide which hill you would like to die on. In other words what are the consequences of going to the next level.

The leader must determine if their values are being compromised by the bosses behavior. Is the leaders integrity being compromised? Can the team continue to function effectively without the the support leader's boss? Every leader should ask these questions before making the decision to go to the next level.

If the need warrants go all the way to the top. Once you pick your battle be prepared to fight your way to a successful conclusion. Don't back down. If the need is great you have nothing to lose.

Remember, everyone has a boss. The question that remains.....Is it worth the fight?

Rule # 23

Counseling does not have to be adversarial?

If you mention the word counseling, most people will see it as a negative experience. This is due to the fact that many people have been in a so called "counseling session" in which they received one sided negative feedback. Or maybe they were yelled at or they were chewed out by a superior. This is not counseling.

Counseling should take place when an employee is off track. They need to be redirected to correct inappropriate behavior. The leader will set down with the individual and develop an action plan to assist in the behavior correction.

Initially there is no disciplinary action taken against the employee (depending on the severity of the behavior). All the leader is attempting to due is work with the employee to get him or her back on track. What could be more positive than helping an individual correct their behavior?

Counseling is just another tool to help employees succeed. If no improvement is seen after the first counseling session disciplinary action may be needed. But the objective is not to punish or discipline. The objective is to change behavior.

Remember, counseling an employee should not be a negative experience. It is a positive behavior modifying session that only becomes negative when the employee refuses to change their behavior.

Rule # 24

Teach yourself out of a job!

It doesn't sound logical to teach yourself out of a job. But that's what effective leaders do. They teach the people the leadership skills needed to move up in rank or authority.

A good leader does not want to see the organization fail once they leave the leadership position. They have worked hard to bring the organization to a new level. Continued success is the leaders main concern.

To assure this success the leaders will share their knowledge and skills. They develop the people so there are many that are ready to take over the reins of the organization.

Growing people is a positive reflection on the leader. And if the leader is doing a good job developing people, there will always be a place for the leader, either in the current organization or another organization.

People notice leaders that develop leaders. Organizations seek out leaders that develop leaders. The leader that is successfully developing the people will be in high demand. Developing people is an asset that is lacking in many organizations. Go against the norm and help people learn what you know.

Remember, your #1 goal as a leader is to help people succeed. So, teach them sound leadership principles.

Rule # 25

Leadership is not about ego!

Leadership is not about ego. It's about a privilege that should be embraced. The privilege is not about being above the rules, instead it is about being held to a higher standard than those around you. It means that the leader has more responsibility but very few *rights*.

The leader is not special because of their position. They are special because they choose to lead and they make the organization better by making the people better.

Ego is about "*me*", leadership is about "*we*". Leadership is about working with the people to make the organization better. It's about focusing on what is best for the organization, not what's best for the leader.

Leadership is about maintaining a high level of customer service. It is about doing what's *right* even when it hurts.

Leadership is not about ego. It's about maintaining and promoting a positive attitude. It's about setting a positive tone for the organization.

Leadership is about maintaining a high level of integrity. It's about honesty. It's about being straight forward and not playing games. Leadership is about being trustworthy.

Leadership is not about ego, it's about being humble and giving credit for success to the people.

-NOTES-

-NOTES-

-NOTES-

-NOTES-

About The Author

As a speaker and seminar leader, Tim has conducted programs throughout the United States. He specializes in helping individuals and organizations maximize their potential.

Tim graduated with honors from Ottawa University in Kansas. He has an extensive background in health care management, the fire service, and organizational development. He is Chief of the German Township Fire & EMS (Clark County, Ohio) and a member of the International Association of Fire Chiefs and Ohio Fire Chiefs.

As a member of the National Speakers Association, Tim is frequently requested to speak at conferences and retreats across the country. He is known for presenting highly unique and motivating programs that give practical solutions to today's hectic and demanding world.

Tim has written numerous articles for national journals and he has published two other books, *The Ten Commandments Of Highly Successful Leaders* (Morris Publishing), *The Building Blocks Of A Winning Team* (Morris Publishing).

Tim resides in West Central Ohio with his wife Becky and their two daughters.

If you would like information on additional books or seminars contact us at:

Tim L. Holman
PO Box 353
North Hampton, Ohio 45349

(937)964-1534

email: htdholman@donet.com

Leadership Rules of Engagement Order Form

Use this convenient order form to order additional copies
of
Leadership Rules of Engagement

Please Print:

Name_____

Address_____

City_____ **State**_____

Zip_____

Phone(**)**_____

_____ copies of book @ $ 5.00 each $ _____
Postage and handling @ $1.95 per book $ _____
OH residents add 6% tax $ _____
Total amount enclosed $ _____

Make checks payable to Tim L. Holman

*Send to Tim L. Holman
P. O. Box 353 • North Hampton • OH • 45349*